MW01252712

33709 0064 9968 2

VIRTUAL FIELD TRIPS

THE STATUE OF LIBERTY
AND
ELLIS ISLAND
A MyReportLinks.com Book

Joseph D. Faria

MyReportLinks.com Books
an imprint of

 Enslow Publishers, Inc.
Box 398, 40 Industrial Road
Berkeley Heights, NJ 07922
USA

Dedication

To Michele—my best friend and my true love. This work is as much from your mind as it is from mine . . . if not more so. Our first publication!

MyReportLinks.com Books, an imprint of Enslow Publishers, Inc. MyReportLinks® is a registered trademark of Enslow Publishers, Inc.

Copyright © 2005 by Enslow Publishers, Inc.

Library of Congress Cataloging-in-Publication Data

Faria, Joseph D.
  The Statue of Liberty and Ellis Island / Joseph D. Faria.
      p. cm. — (Virtual field trips)
  Includes bibliographical references and index.
  ISBN 0-7660-5226-5
  1. Statue of Liberty (New York, N.Y.)—Juvenile literature. 2. Statue of Liberty National
Monument (N.Y. and N.J.)—Juvenile literature. [1. Ellis Island Immigration Station (N.Y. and N.J.)
—Juvenile literature. 2. United States—Emigration and immigration—History—Juvenile literature.] I.
Title. II. Series.
  F128.64.L6F37 2005
  325.73—dc22
                                    2004013516

Printed in the United States of America

10 9 8 7 6 5 4 3 2 1

To Our Readers:
Through the purchase of this book, you and your library gain access to the Report Links that specifically back up this book.
The Publisher will provide access to the Report Links that back up this book and will keep these Report Links up to date on **www.myreportlinks.com** for five years from the book's first publication date.
We have done our best to make sure all Internet addresses in this book were active and appropriate when we went to press. However, the author and the Publisher have no control over, and assume no liability for, the material available on those Internet sites or on other Web sites they may link to.
The usage of the MyReportLinks.com Books Web site is subject to the terms and conditions stated on the Usage Policy Statement on **www.myreportlinks.com**.
A password may be required to access the Report Links that back up this book. The password is found on the bottom of page 4 of this book.
Any comments or suggestions can be sent by e-mail to comments@myreportlinks.com or to the address on the back cover.

Photo Credits: © 1995 PhotoDisc, pp. 3, 36; © 2000 The Statue of Liberty-Ellis Island Foundation, Inc., p. 12; © 2002 Aramark Sports and Entertainment, Inc., p. 38; © 2004 Discovery Communications, Inc., pp. 24, 28, 35; © 2004 Jewish Women's Archive, p. 33; © Corel Corporation, p. 1 (background image of statue); Library of Congress, p. 1 (Ellis Island), 9, 14, 15, 18, 20, 21, 26, 32, 39; MyReportLinks.com Books, p. 4; National Park Service, pp. 22, 40; National Park Service: Statue of Liberty National Monument, pp. 16, 27, 30; Photos.com, pp. 1 (crown and moon), 10, 42.

Cover Photo: © 1995 PhotoDisc, (Great Hall); © Corel Corporation; Enslow Publishers, Inc.

Cover Description: In the background is the Great Hall at Ellis Island. A silhouette of the Statue of Liberty is in front on the left. The underside of the New York state quarter is on the top bar.

Report Links 4

Statue of Liberty and
Ellis Island Facts 9

1▷ Coming to America 10

2▷ History of Ellis Island 15

3▷ History of the Statue of Liberty 22

4▷ Ellis Island Today 36

5▷ The Statue of Liberty Today 40

Glossary 44

Chapter Notes 45

Further Reading 47

Index 48

MyReportLinks.com Books
Great Books, Great Links, Great for Research!

The Internet sites listed on the next four pages can save you hours of research time. These Internet sites—we call them "Report Links"—are constantly changing, but we keep them up to date on our Web site.

Give it a try! Type http://www.myreportlinks.com into your browser, click on the series title, then the book title, and scroll down to the Report Links listed for this book.

The Report Links will bring you to great source documents, photographs, and illustrations. MyReportLinks.com Books save you time, feature Report Links that are kept up to date, and make report writing easier than ever!

Please see "To Our Readers" on the copyright page for important information about this book, the MyReportLinks.com Web site, and the Report Links that back up this book.

Please enter **FTL1448** if asked for a password.

Report Links

The Internet sites described below can be accessed at http://www.myreportlinks.com

*EDITOR'S CHOICE

▶Statue of Liberty National Monument
The National Park Service Web site has a vast amount of information about the Statue of Liberty. Click on "In Depth" to read more about this national monument.

*EDITOR'S CHOICE

▶Ellis Island National Monument
Almost everything you need to know about Ellis Island can be found at its National Park Service Web site.

*EDITOR'S CHOICE

▶Ellis Island
Get a glimpse of what immigrants experienced while they were at Ellis Island at this interactive Web site. Listen to personal stories, view the different stages the immigrants went through, and answer the questions that most immigrants had to answer.

*EDITOR'S CHOICE

▶American Icons: Lady Liberty
On this Web site from the Travel Channel, you can learn about the Statue of Liberty, as well as hear personal stories from five immigrants who passed through Ellis Island in the 1920s.

*EDITOR'S CHOICE

▶American Stories: The Statue of Liberty
You can explore the history of the Statue of Liberty at this PBS Web site. View images, time lines, and much more.

*EDITOR'S CHOICE

▶Ellis Island History
This Web site contains a brief history of Ellis Island. You will also find a time line and learn about the immigrant experience.

Report Links

The Internet sites described below can be accessed at http://www.myreportlinks.com

▶ **Celebrating the Immigrant**

At this National Park Service Web site you can read about the immigrant experience as it is retold by author Barbara Bloomberg.

▶ **Ellis & Liberty Islands**

The Ellis & Liberty Islands Web site allows you to view a time line and map, and read stories from the ancestors of immigrants.

▶ **Ellis Island: National Park Service**

This Web site provides a brief history of Ellis Island and information on the many programs and museum exhibits at this national monument.

▶ **Emma Lazarus**

A brief biography of Emma Lazarus, the author of "The New Colossus," can be found here. In 1903, this poem was inscribed on a bronze plaque placed on the pedestal of the Statue of Liberty. Click on "Forward" to read the poem.

▶ **The First Immigrant Landed on Ellis Island January 1, 1892**

America's Story from America's Library, a Library of Congress Web site, describes the process of entering the United States through Ellis Island.

▶ **History, Genealogy, and Education**

At this Web site, learn about immigration, green cards, immigration archival records, and other useful information.

▶ **History of Ellis Island**

The American Park Network provides a brief history of Ellis Island. Topics covered include its construction and reconstruction, immigration laws, and more.

▶ **History of Quarantine**

Sick immigrants coming into Ellis Island were often quarantined. Read about the prevention of the spread of diseases in the United States.

Report Links

The Internet sites described below can be accessed at http://www.myreportlinks.com

▶**Immigrant Life in New York City**

Immigrants often lived in cheap apartments in New York City after arriving in the United States. This online resource describes the tenements in New York City and the Lower East Side Tenement Museum.

▶**Immigrants to United States by Country of Origin**

Infoplease.com lists immigration statistics from 1820 to 1996.

▶**Learning Adventures in Citizenship**

At PBS's Learning Adventures in Citizenship Web site, you can learn about hardships in American life from 1609 to the present, including immigration to the United States.

▶**New York, NY, Ellis Island—Immigration: 1900–1920**

View many images of Ellis Island taken during its years of operation. They are online at this Web site.

▶**The Restoration of Ellis Island**

Find out about the project to restore Ellis Island. View before and after images of the project.

▶**Selected Images of Ellis Island and Immigration, ca. 1880–1920**

At this Library of Congress Web site you can explore images of Ellis Island.

▶**Selected Views of the Statue of Liberty**

This Library of Congress Web site provides images of the Statue of Liberty, from its construction to the time it first stood tall in the New York Harbor.

▶**Statue of Liberty**

Edouard de Laboulaye was a French historian and supporter of American government. Learn more about the man whose idea it was to give the Statue of Liberty to the United States to commemorate the country's independence.

Report Links

The Internet sites described below can be accessed at http://www.myreportlinks.com

▶Statue of Liberty: History

Read about where the idea for the Statue of Liberty came from, as well as a biography of Frédéric-Auguste Bartholdi, the sculptor who created it.

▶The Statue of Liberty Arrived in New York Harbor

This site from the Library of Congress details the arrival of the Statue of Liberty in the United States. There is also a link to Thomas Edison's movie footage of the statue.

▶Statue of Liberty Facts

Learn interesting facts about the Statue of Liberty, from the size of her hand to the length of her sandal and more.

▶The Statue of Liberty National Monument

The American Park Network Web site tells the story of Annie Moore, the first immigrant to pass through Ellis Island.

▶The Statue of Liberty Photo Tour

NYCTourist.com provides a photo tour of the Statue of Liberty. Climb to the top for an amazing view.

▶The Statue of Liberty-Ellis Island Foundation, Inc.

At the Statue of Liberty-Ellis Island Foundation Web site, you can read about those who passed through Ellis Island, the immigrant experience, and much more.

▶Today in History: Statue of Liberty

Learn about the arrival of the Statue of Liberty in New York at this Library of Congress Web site.

▶Walking Onto Ellis Island, New York

America's Story from America's Library, a Library of Congress Web site, tells about those immigrants passing through Ellis Island.

Statue of Liberty and Ellis Island Facts

- The Statue of Liberty is one of the largest and most recognizable pieces of artwork ever created. It has been pictured on the cover of such magazines as *The New Yorker, Life,* and *National Geographic.*

- The official title of the Statue of Liberty is "Liberty Enlightening the World."

- Alexandre Gustave Eiffel, the structural engineer responsible for Paris's Eiffel Tower, designed the framework for the Statue of Liberty.

- Thomas Edison's motion picture company filmed the Statue of Liberty twelve years after its arrival in America. The film, titled *Statue of Liberty,* is available online or at most local libraries.

- The Statue of Liberty is located on Liberty Island in New York Harbor but lies within the borders of Jersey City, New Jersey.[1] However, Liberty Island is actually the property of the federal government within the jurisdiction of the state of New York.

- The federal government purchased Ellis Island from the heirs of Samuel Ellis for ten thousand dollars.

- Four out of ten Americans can trace their heritage through Ellis Island.[2]

- Thousands of marriages were performed at Ellis Island at the "Kissing Post," a spot where families who had been separated were reunited with their loved ones.[3]

- Some famous people who entered the United States through Ellis Island include movie director Frank Capra, comedian Bob Hope, actor Bela Lugosi, and scientist and author Isaac Asimov.

- Both Liberty Island and Ellis Island were once the home of military forts. Fort Wood was located on Liberty Island, and Fort Gibson was on Ellis Island. The forts no longer function, but some of their structures remain.

Processing at Ellis Island. ▶

Coming to America

The giant figure came slowly into view, a shining image standing proudly out of the fog. From the crowded deck below, it looked as if her head was politely inclined to welcome the travel-weary passengers on the steamship.

The travelers turned their hopeful eyes up to take in the great torch. It was brightly held aloft like a message to the heavens that all was well under the peaceful gray sky of the harbor. The journey from Europe had taken what seemed like forever, but the passengers felt an excitement they had not felt for weeks stirring inside of them as they caught their first glimpse of the majestic statue.

The ship stopped, and the excited people moved as one toward the port side. Their long voyage should have used up most of their energy, but gazing up at the lady among

Despite the closing of Ellis Island as an immigration station, the Statue of Liberty still waits in New York Harbor to greet immigrants as they enter the United States.

the billowing fog had given them renewed vigor. Suddenly, the sky before them was lit with a proud fire as the torch the statue held was illuminated. The passengers felt a rush of joy come surging through them. The faces in the crowd were smiling and animated—faces that had been drawn and mostly silent for the duration of the journey.

As the fog moved along over the harbor, the silvery-black backdrop of New York City completed the scene, like a gateway to a mythic land. The travelers had arrived on an important day in the life of the Statue of Liberty. It was October 28, 1886, the day of the long-awaited celebration to dedicate the statue. With smiles that foretold their expectations for the future, the travelers awaited the ferry bound for the immigration station—and the beginning of their new lives in the United States of America.

Ellis Island Immigration

Ellis Island is a small island located in New York Harbor. It is about a half mile from Liberty Island, the island upon which the Statue of Liberty stands. During a sixty-year period, from January 1892 to November 1954, more than 12 million people came through Ellis Island on their way into the United States.[1] Some left their homes to escape war or persecution for their religious beliefs. Others were searching for a better life or were driven by stories that said that in America hard work was rewarded with prosperity. Still others wanted their children to grow up in a country where freedom was a way of life instead of an unattainable dream. Not every person who arrived at Ellis Island, though, was admitted into the United States. About 2 percent—which, at times, could be up to a thousand people a month—of the hopeful immigrants who stepped onto the shores of New York's welcoming center were deported back to their homelands.

Sometimes, immigrants were sent back for health reasons. Public Health Service doctors quickly checked each person standing in line for signs of diseases such as cholera, favus (a type of fungus that affects the scalp and nails), tuberculosis, or trachoma

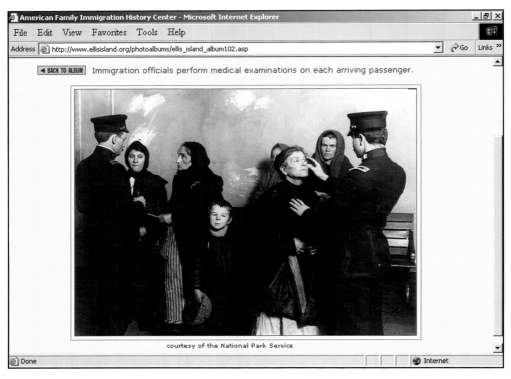

American Family Immigration History Center - Microsoft Internet Explorer

File Edit View Favorites Tools Help

Address http://www.ellisisland.org/photoalbums/ellis_island_album102.asp   Go Links »

◄ BACK TO ALBUM   Immigration officials perform medical examinations on each arriving passenger.

courtesy of the National Park Service

Done   Internet

Doctors checked every immigrant passing through Ellis Island for eye infections, lameness, and mental disturbances. If an immigrant displayed symptoms of any of these, they were given a more specialized examination, sometimes resulting in hospitalization or quarantine.

(an extremely contagious eye infection that results in blindness or even death).[2] These inspections came to be known as the "six-second physical." In addition, an immigrant could be denied entry into the United States if doctors suspected that he or she was deaf, mute, or mentally disabled.

About nine out of every hundred immigrants were detained for mental examination and further questioning. Usually this consisted of standard intelligence tests in which immigrants were asked to solve simple arithmetic problems, count backwards from twenty, or complete a puzzle. In an attempt to deal with immigrants' cultural differences, Ellis Island's doctors developed their own tests, which allowed them to base their decision on problem solving, behavior, attitude, and the immigrant's ability to acquire knowledge. Requiring immigrants to copy geometric shapes, for instance, was only useful for testing those who had some schooling and were used to holding a pencil. Favored were comparisons and mimicry tests, which did not have to be explained by an interpreter, nor did an immigrant have to know how to read and write to solve them.[3]

Other times, authorities at Ellis Island were concerned that some immigrants would be unable to support themselves or would exhibit criminal behavior. Before they were allowed entry into the United States, immigrants had to answer questions such as:

"Have you ever been imprisoned?"

"Are you an anarchist [someone who opposes any type of government]?"

"Are you in possession of at least fifty dollars?"

"Do you have a job waiting for you?"[4]

If potential immigrants were unable to respond to these questions with acceptable answers, they were detained, or held, for a special hearing. These hearings were conducted by the Board of Special Inquiry. Although the immigrants could not have a lawyer present, friends or family members could testify on their behalf.[5]

The inspection process at Ellis Island took an average of five hours. Full names were recorded for each arrival, but due to human error as well as translation problems, many immigrants left their homes with one name and arrived in America with another. The American government provided interpreters, but there was often confusion because names were illegible on the ships' documentation, the immigrants were tired or nervous, or they did not fully understand what they were being asked. The inspectors were busy and often looked to simplify names to speed the process

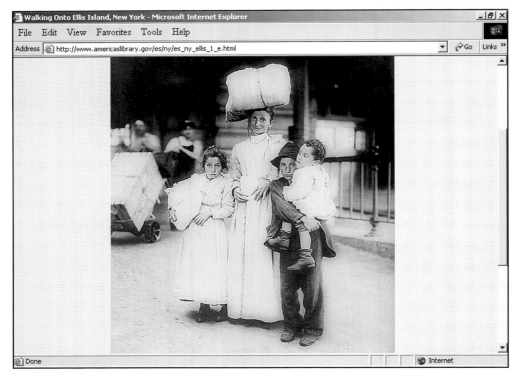

△ A family of Italian immigrants arrives at Ellis Island.

along. So, when someone arrived with a complicated foreign last name and could not communicate well enough to spell it out, an inspector would often shorten, or "Americanize," the name.[6]

Details such as each immigrant's nationality, age, marital status, and destination were also recorded, in addition to information such as whether the person was literate, how the passage to America was financed, how much money he or she had, whether a relative was meeting him or her in America, and other personal questions.[7] When the exhaustive process finally ended, the great majority of those who arrived hopefully on the shores of America in search of religious freedom, financial opportunities, and a better quality of living were free to make their way forward into a life full of promise and fulfillment.

History of Ellis Island

Ellis Island was not always a place to welcome weary travelers. Once, it was a place where oysters were farmed, ammunition was stored, and even a place where pirates were hanged. A look back into the history of Ellis Island helps us to see how it came to be the way it presently is.

In the 1600s, Chippewa Indians called the island *Kioshk,* which means Gull Island, because of the great number of seagulls living there.[1] The gulls, however, were not the only living things on the island. When a Dutch settler, Michael Paauw, purchased

▲ Ellis Island was purchased by the United States government in 1808 to house Fort Gibson, an ammunition arsenal. This fort was eventually knocked down to build the immigration station (shown here), which opened on January 1, 1892.

Kioshk from the American Indians on July 12, 1630, he soon discovered the oysters buried in the sand there. The new owner then changed the name, appropriately, to Oyster Island. Because the island was bought and sold again many times, the island's name changed several more times. In 1765, for example, the island was renamed—this time, it was called Gibbet Island. A "gibbet" is the gallows used to execute criminals. Pirates were often hanged using this method on Gibbet Island.[2]

▲ Annie Moore, an Irish teenager, was the first immigrant to be admitted to Ellis Island. She had traveled from Ireland with her two brothers to be reunited with her parents who had arrived three years earlier. A grown-up Moore poses circa 1910 with her first American-born child, Mary Catherine.

In the late 1770s, a man named Samuel Ellis became the owner, and the island was named after him.[3] In 1808, the island was purchased by the government of the United States. The government built a fort there, which they named Fort Gibson after a fallen soldier. Fort Gibson on Ellis Island was used by the military for some time as a place to store ammunition and to imprison criminals.

▶ An Immigration Station

It was not until January 1, 1892, that Ellis Island began its sixty-two-year function as an immigration station. The island was only 3 acres in size and set in shallow water, which sometimes made it difficult for boats to access. Yet a congressional committee had chosen the island as an ideal place to process the thousands of immigrants who were arriving each month. Among other reasons, Ellis Island was chosen because military weapons and explosives were stored at Fort Gibson. Many people were worried about such dangerous things being stored so close to the cities of New York and New Jersey.[4] Residents knew that once the immigration station at Ellis Island was officially planned, the explosives would be removed from the island.

For nearly two years and with a budget of $500,000, workers enlarged Ellis Island. They built docks and constructed wooden buildings to serve as a registration hall, inspection center, hospital, laundry room, and a utility plant. The naval barracks that had originally stood on the island were converted to dormitories. On New Year's Day 1892, Ellis Island was formally opened as an immigration station.

The first person to be admitted to the new immigration station was a fifteen-year-old Irish girl named Annie Moore. She had come to America on board the steamship *Nevada* and was one of 148 steerage passengers who had been eager for the honor of being the first to land at Ellis Island. Annie Moore was the first to enter the United States through an immigration process that the other

445,987 immigrants who passed through Ellis Island that year would also follow.

Although the plans for Ellis Island had been carefully carried out, some complications eventually arose. In 1897, for example, the structure used for processing the immigrants caught fire and burned to the ground. No lives had been lost in the fire, but some of the immigration records dating back to 1840 were. Following this, the government decided that only fireproof buildings were to be built on Ellis Island. So on December 17, 1900, a new processing building made of brick and limestone over a steel frame, was opened. The other structures were rebuilt as well, and a restaurant and bathhouse were added.

In addition, although the island had been enlarged prior to the opening of its function as an immigration station, it had not been made large enough. Between 1900 and 1914, one million immigrants a year entered the United States through Ellis Island.

New York, Ellis Island.

▲ Immigrants disembarking from the ferry walk across the dock to Ellis Island. There they will undergo several medical examinations before being allowed passage into the United States.

This forced the government to accommodate the ever-growing numbers by enlarging the island from 3 acres to 27 acres. Dirt that had been removed during construction of the New York City subway system was used to add land mass to the island's original size.

Arriving at Ellis Island

Passengers who journeyed to America by ship did not sail directly to Ellis Island. Before passengers could reach the island, immigrant ships were stopped at the Coast Guard's Quarantine Station in the Narrows off Staten Island. The Narrows is a strip of water that separates Staten Island from Brooklyn. Officers would board the ships and check the people for diseases before they would allow them to proceed. Ships were then docked at the Hudson River or East River piers, and passengers were brought by ferry to Ellis Island.

Once they made it to Ellis Island, immigrants had to undergo detailed physical and mental examinations. Doctors would scrutinize the physical health of each individual, checking for issues such as eye infections, lameness, or mental disturbances. As these conditions were spotted, people were brought elsewhere for a more specialized examination, which sometimes resulted in hospitalization or quarantine. Others were given simple tests that were designed to reflect their logic skills, the results of which would determine whether they were sent back to their country of origin.

First- and second-class travelers, who could afford the better accommodations on the ship, did not have to endure the inspections that the steerage passengers had to submit to. The government felt that immigrants who could afford such a ticket would not become a burden on the country. It did not want to allow into the country people that were likely to become homeless and that the state would have to pay to care for. However, if first- or second-class passengers showed obvious signs of illness, they still had to go through the inspection process.[5]

If it was determined that an immigrant was physically and mentally healthy, he or she would proceed to the Registry Room,

Immigrants wait to be examined by Ellis Island physicians. Despite a brief medical examination, the average inspection process for an immigrant lasted five hours if his or her papers were in order and he or she was in good health.

also known as the Great Hall. Once there, the immigrant would prove to the inspectors that he or she had some money to begin his or her new life. The inspectors also wanted to see letters from relatives who were waiting in America for the newcomer.

"Moral" qualifications were required for processing, as well: Single women were not permitted to leave the island unless it was with a family member, so many couples decided to get married on the spot with immigration inspectors acting as witnesses. Eventually, however, this practice was discontinued and couples who wished to marry were brought to New York's City Hall.[6]

During its time of operation, Ellis Island was the start of a new life for some and the end of life for others. Out of all the arrivals over the sixty-two years Ellis Island operated, some 3,500 died on the island, 350 babies were born, and 3 people committed suicide.[7] While tragedy did sometimes occur and while the immigration experience was often a very difficult time, Ellis Island was indeed the beginning of a positive new era in the lives of many individuals and families.

Ellis Island Closes

Although most tried to maintain a professional courtesy to the immigrants, the staff who had been employed throughout the peak years of the island—doctors, interpreters, nurses, inspectors, etc.—were beginning to feel overwhelmed. The total number

In 1964, Stewart Udall, interior secretary under President Lyndon B. Johnson, visited Ellis Island. Recognizing its historical significance, he persuaded the president to make it part of the Statue of Liberty National Monument.

of staff members was around 250, and they had to attend to 230 detainees (immigrants suspected of mental deficiencies) per day, not to mention regulate the inspection and processing of incoming immigrants.

After 1924, the number of immigrants dropped to fewer than 190,000 per year.[8] The cost of operating Ellis Island was great, and immigration laws were becoming more strictly enforced. An immigration station at Ellis Island was no longer needed. So on November 12, 1954, the doors to Ellis Island's immigration station finally closed. Arne Peterssen, a Norwegian seaman who had not returned to his fleet on time, was the last detainee in Ellis Island's history. Without ceremony, Peterssen was granted parole and given passage to the mainland.[9]

After the doors were closed, the General Services Administration put Ellis Island up for sale. People interested in buying the island wanted to turn it into a women's prison, a casino, a slaughterhouse, or an amusement park. None of their offers was accepted.

Eleven years later, Stewart Udall, the secretary of the interior in then-president Lyndon B. Johnson's administration, recognized the island's symbolic importance to America. He convinced President Johnson to proclaim Ellis Island a part of the Statue of Liberty National Monument in 1965. Ellis Island was taken under the care of the National Park Service, part of the United States Department of the Interior.[10]

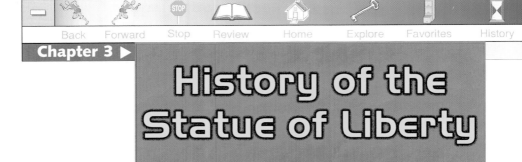

Chapter 3

History of the
Statue of Liberty

Friendship between France and the United States of America has existed since the United States was first established. In fact, without France's aid, the United States probably would not have won its freedom from British rule during the Revolutionary War (1775–83).[1] During France's conflict with

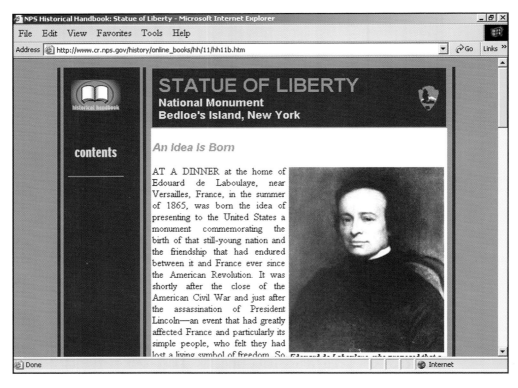

▲ Edouard de Laboulaye, a French historian, believed strongly that the friendship between the United States and France should be honored. It was his idea for France to give a monument to the United States to commemorate a century of American independence.

Germany during the Franco-Prussian War in 1870, America sent provisions to Paris in its time of need. The two countries were united in a bond that included a mutual regard for freedom and a mutual feeling of respect.

A French professor named Edouard-Rene Lefebvre de Laboulaye was the person who came up with the idea of honoring the United States with the Statue of Liberty. De Laboulaye proposed the idea at one of his gatherings in the summer of 1865, but it was not until some time later that his idea for a gift to America began to come to life. Laboulaye's goal was to bring the countries of France and United States closer together, as well as to give the young nation a present to commemorate the celebration of the one-hundredth anniversary of the Declaration of Independence in 1876. However, this deadline did not prove to be possible.

A Large Undertaking

A successful young French sculptor named Frédéric-Auguste Bartholdi was chosen to undertake the task of creating a giant statue for America. As a soldier in the Franco-Prussian War, Bartholdi had learned firsthand the repercussions of an oppressive force, as his homeland of Alsace had been lost to Prussia. This made him enthusiastic about participating in the new project. French citizens, eager to do their part, donated money to be used in the construction of the statue.

Bartholdi felt that the monument should be large. He had always favored sculpting massive and broad forms that could be seen as chiseled silhouettes from a distance. Bartholdi was inspired by various pieces of art. These include the equestrian statue of Peter the Great in St. Petersburg, Russia, and a statue standing on the Bastille (a French prison) called the Genius of Liberty. This figure carried a torch in one hand and a broken chain in the other.

Many of the grand buildings in America also captivated his imagination: Thomas Jefferson's home, Monticello; George Washington's home, Mount Vernon; and various buildings in

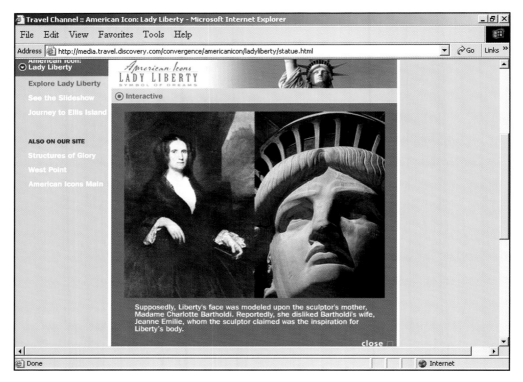

File   Edit   View   Favorites   Tools   Help

Address http://media.travel.discovery.com/convergence/americanicon/ladyliberty/statue.html

American Icon:
Lady Liberty

Explore Lady Liberty

See the Slideshow

Journey to Ellis Island

ALSO ON OUR SITE

Structures of Glory

West Point

American Icons Main

American Icons
LADY LIBERTY
SYMBOL OF DREAMS

Interactive

Supposedly, Liberty's face was modeled upon the sculptor's mother, Madame Charlotte Bartholdi. Reportedly, she disliked Bartholdi's wife, Jeanne Emilie, whom the sculptor claimed was the inspiration for Liberty's body.

close

Done   Internet

▲ *Although it is commonly believed that Madame Charlotte Bartholdi, the designer's mother, was the model for the Statue of Liberty's face, some believe otherwise.*

Washington, D.C. He began to wonder if the form of a woman would be ideal to represent freedom and liberty. There were already some such representations in existence, such as the painting "Liberty Leading the People" by Eugene Delacroix. This painting was of a young woman holding a flag and a musket, leading revolutionaries. In addition, there was the unofficial symbol of America—a woman wearing a robe.[2]

Designing the Statue

Many speculative stories surround the origin of the striking face of the Statue of Liberty, but no one really knows for certain who actually modeled for Bartholdi. A young French model named Jeanne-Emile Baheux, whom he eventually married, was rumored to have been the inspiration for the statue's face. She, however, was not in France when Bartholdi was designing the statue. She was living in America, which means that it is unlikely for her to have been the model for the face.[3]

What is popularly believed is that Bartholdi's mother was his inspiration for the statue's regal facial features. Bartholdi admitted as much when he spoke to a French senator at an opera house, but no one person was ever officially named as the model for the face of the Statue of Liberty.[4]

The Statue's Designer Visits America

Frédéric-Auguste Bartholdi decided that he needed to visit America so that he could capture the spirit of the young country— and perhaps persuade it to accept his Statue of Liberty. When he arrived in New York Harbor in June 1871, Bartholdi instantly envisioned his soon-to-be statue standing tall on Bedloe's Island greeting all the weary immigrants at Ellis Island. Fort Wood was located on Bedloe's Island. Although Bedloe's Island was being used by the military for the defense of New York, Bartholdi hoped that it would become the home of the Statue of Liberty. He felt this way even before he landed on the shores of the United States. Looking out at New York from his ship, Bartholdi wrote:

> The picture that is presented to the view when one arrives in New York is marvelous, when, after some days of voyaging, in the pearly radiance of a beautiful morning is revealed the magnificent spectacle of those immense cities, of those rivers extending as far as the eye can reach, festooned with masts and flags; when one awakes, so to speak, in the midst of that interior sea covered with vessels . . . it is thrilling. It is, indeed, the New World, which appears in its majestic expanse, with the ardor of its glowing life.

MyReportLinks.com Books

THE BARTHOLDI COLOSSAL STATUE,

▲ *Frédéric-Auguste Bartholdi envisioned the Statue of Liberty as a greeting for those immigrating to the United States. He created the statue as a tribute to American independence and democracy.*

Bartholdi later discovered that Bedloe's Island was owned by the federal government, which made it the property of all the states. He felt even more certain that this was the perfect site for his statue because it would then be set on land commonly owned by all of the United States.[6]

▶ Construction of the Statue and Pedestal

Once he knew how massive the statue would be, Bartholdi needed to decide the best material for its construction. Because it is lightweight, easy to work with, and relatively inexpensive, copper seemed to be the best choice. Copper sheets about the thickness of two pennies were wrapped around a frame made up of compartments filled with sand. (The reason for this type of inner frame was so that if repairs needed to be made on the statue, a section could be isolated, drained of the sand, and worked on without disturbing the rest of the structure.)[7]

Constructing a monument of this type was a large—and expensive—undertaking. In 1875, the French-American Union was established to raise money and oversee the project. Laboulaye was the chairman of the organization in France. The French people donated $400,000 for the construction of the statue.

In 1877, the American Committee was organized in the United States to raise funds to build the pedestal upon which the completed statue would stand. The estimate for the construction of the pedestal was originally $125,000, and contributions were barely trickling in.

▲ *Bartholdi works on the statue's hand. Although it appears enormous, the Statue of Liberty stands only 151 feet tall. The height more than doubles to 305 feet when you include the pedestal, but the statue is small when compared to more modern structures such as New York's Empire State Building.*

Despite financial worries, however, the committee appointed one of the most famous American architects of the day, Richard Morris Hunt, to design the pedestal upon the foundation of the star-shaped fort that was built on Bedloe's Island. Hunt wrote a letter to Bartholdi, asking him for detailed specifications as to the size of the statue. After receiving this information, Hunt drew up detailed sketches and calculations and discovered that the result would cost a good deal more than the original estimate. Money was still coming in slowly, and now the committee needed even more to fulfill their dreams of the statue standing tall in New York Harbor.

In November 1882, the committee sponsored a "monster mass meeting" at the Academy of Music, which featured a model

▲ America had a difficult time raising the money needed to build the Statue of Liberty's pedestal. Part of the fund-raising effort at the 1876 Philadelphia Centennial included the chance to walk up the statue's right arm containing the torch in exchange for a small donation.

of the statue and a painting of the statue by famous artist Edward Moran. The audience was shocked to hear that the pedestal that would hold the Statue of Liberty was now expected to cost $250,000 and that the committee had only collected $75,000. This was a very large amount of money for that time, but it was still far less than was needed.

Joseph Pulitzer, who established the fund that awards the annual Pulitzer Prize for literature, drama, music, and journalism, stepped in to help with the effort to raise money for the pedestal. Pulitzer's newspaper, the *New York World*, ran headlines and editorials criticizing Americans for not donating to the construction of the pedestal that would hold the Statue of Liberty.[8] Pulitzer also began a campaign to accept donations of any amount. Although the campaign was not immediately a success and was dropped for a time, it would have dramatic results when it was begun again two years later.

▶ The Statue Is Completed

The final construction on the Statue of Liberty was completed in France, in July 1884. The French-American Union sent a notice that the statue was finished and awaited word from America that the pedestal was ready. Since the pedestal fund was still far short of its goal, the Franco-American Union created a collection of art that had never before been seen in public exhibition. They hoped that the money raised by the Bartholdi Statue Pedestal Fund Art Loan Exhibition would be enough to complete the pedestal. Although the twelve thousand dollars raised by the exhibition was helpful, it was still not enough. Two days after the exhibition closed, they learned that an additional $175,000 was needed to finish the project.[9]

The Sons of the American Revolution, a patriotic organization in the United States, announced that it would be a national disgrace if construction on the pedestal failed. Fund-raising rallies were sponsored, but the committee was far from the amount it needed. Finally, other cities, such as Baltimore, Maryland; Boston, Massachusetts; Philadelphia, Pennsylvania; and San Francisco, California; began expressing their interest in housing the statue, saying that New York clearly did not deserve the honor since the contributions were not being made.

▲ French sculptor Frédéric-Auguste Bartholdi, shown here in his Paris studio, created the Statue of Liberty.

Once again, Joseph Pulitzer stepped in. On March 14, 1885, he published an editorial in *New York World* that he titled "The National Disgrace." He asked that his readers donate "something, however little," and promised that the newspaper would "publish the name of every giver, however small the sum given."[10] This proved to be the effort the committee was waiting for, because many people wanted to contribute so that they could see their names in print. The people sprang into action and donated whatever they could afford—a dollar here, ten cents there—to build the pedestal. Although this may not seem like much today, in 1885 many people had a salary of around five dollars a month. Still, they sent what they could to give the Statue of Liberty a home.

By August 11, 1885, the grand total had been reached. The *New York World* ran a headline boasting that $100,000 had been raised, along with a front-page article with a sketch of the statue holding the American flag next to her torch. In just five months, the remainder of the money had been raised. Eighty percent of the total had been received in sums of less than a dollar.[11]

Lady Liberty: Home at Last

The people of France had proudly presented the Statue of Liberty to the citizens of the United States of America. Now, the more than 150-foot-tall symbol of freedom had to be transported to its rightful place on Bedloe's Island at the entrance to the harbor.

On January 1, 1885, the Statue of Liberty was disassembled into 350 pieces and packed into 214 crates. The weight of each box varied significantly: some were 150 pounds; some were 3 tons. A train of seventy cars brought the boxes to the French warship *Isere*.[12] There, the boxes were numbered in order and loaded so that the pieces necessary for initial assembly were packed last and would be unpacked first. With all the careful preparations, it was not until May 21, 1885, that the *Isere* and her escort ship, *Flore*, finally set sail for America. The *Isere* arrived bearing the Statue of Liberty on June 17, 1885.[13]

On October 28, 1886, the celebration to dedicate the Statue of Liberty was held. There was a parade and a twenty-one-gun salute. Over a million spectators turned up for the event. It was a proud day in the history of the United States that was made even more special for a group of European immigrants who had arrived in America on that very day. From the deck of their steamship, they watched as "the cannon smoke and vapor rolled up, and ringed in a huge, fire-fringed semi-circle, they saw before them the mighty figure of Liberty."[14]

▶ A National Monument

In 1924, the Statue of Liberty was established as a national monument. The National Park Service took over its management in

Taken from Steamer "Patrol", 28 October, 1886.   Copyright 1887, H. O'Neil, 31 Union Square, New York.

"LIBERTY ENLIGHTENING THE WORLD"
INAUGURATION OF THE BARTHOLDI STATUE, HARBOR OF NEW YORK.
MILITARY AND NAVAL SALUTE, THE PRESIDENT'S ARRIVAL AT LIBERTY ISLAND.

△ *The Statue of Liberty was surrounded in smoke after cannon were shot in celebration of her unveiling on October 28, 1886.*

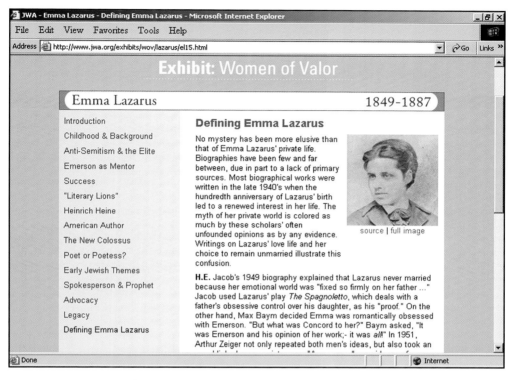

JWA - Emma Lazarus - Defining Emma Lazarus - Microsoft Internet Explorer

File   Edit   View   Favorites   Tools   Help

Address http://www.jwa.org/exhibits/wov/lazarus/el15.html

Exhibit: Women of Valor

Emma Lazarus   1849–1887

Introduction
Childhood & Background
Anti-Semitism & the Elite
Emerson as Mentor
Success
"Literary Lions"
Heinrich Heine
American Author
The New Colossus
Poet or Poetess?
Early Jewish Themes
Spokesperson & Prophet
Advocacy
Legacy
Defining Emma Lazarus

Defining Emma Lazarus

No mystery has been more elusive than that of Emma Lazarus' private life. Biographies have been few and far between, due in part to a lack of primary sources. Most biographical works were written in the late 1940's when the hundredth anniversary of Lazarus' birth led to a renewed interest in her life. The myth of her private world is colored as much by these scholars' often unfounded opinions as by any evidence. Writings on Lazarus' love life and her choice to remain unmarried illustrate this confusion.

source | full image

H.E. Jacob's 1949 biography explained that Lazarus never married because her emotional world was "fixed so firmly on her father ..." Jacob used Lazarus' play *The Spagnoletto*, which deals with a father's obsessive control over his daughter, as his "proof." On the other hand, Max Baym decided Emma was romantically obsessed with Emerson. "But what was Concord to her?" Baym asked, "It was Emerson and his opinion of her work;- it was *all*" In 1951, Arthur Zeiger not only repeated both men's ideas, but also took an

Done   Internet

△ *Emma Lazarus's poem "The New Colossus" was published in 1883 for an art auction called In Aid of the Bartholdi Pedestal Fund. It was not until 1903, sixteen years after the poet's death, that the poem was engraved on a plaque and placed on the Statue of Liberty's pedestal.*

1933. In 1956, Bedloe's Island, where the Statue of Liberty had stood for over seventy years, was renamed "Liberty Island" by an act of Congress.

▷ Symbolism of the Statue of Liberty

When Bartholdi designed the Statue of Liberty, he wanted it to symbolize a variety of things. To represent liberty as "bright enlightenment," he decided that his statue was going to hold a torch in her right hand. Cradled in her left arm would be a tablet inscribed with the date of the Declaration of Independence in

Roman numerals: July IV MDCCLXXVI (July 4, 1776). A seven-pointed crown was decided upon for the statue's head, with each point signifying the seven continents or the seven seas.[15] The broken chains beneath the statue's feet represent freedom from oppression and tyranny.

▶ Chains Crushed Underfoot

If you look at the statue today, you will notice that below, inscribed upon its pedestal, is a poem called "The New Colossus." This poem has become almost as well known as the Statue of Liberty itself. In 1879, violence and anti-Semitism swept over Russia and Eastern Europe. A young Jewish-American writer named Emma Lazarus became very aware of the seriousness of this kind of persecution against her people. She had been asked to write a poem to help raise money for the statue's pedestal.[16] Lazarus based her poem on the great statue of Helios, the Greek god of the sun. This statue is considered one of the Seven Wonders of the Ancient World. Called the Colossus of Rhodes, it stood over two thousand years ago—also at the entrance to a busy harbor— on the Greek Island of Rhodes, an economic hub of the ancient world. Colossus, like the Statue of Liberty, was built as a celebration of freedom.[17] Lazarus's poem reads:

> Not like the brazen giant of Greek fame,
> With conquering limbs astride from land to land;
> Here at our sea-washed, sunset-gates shall stand
> A mighty woman with a torch, whose flame
> Is the imprisoned lightning, and her name
> Mother of Exiles. From her beacon-hand
> Glows world-wide welcome; her mild eyes command
> The air-bridged harbor that twin-cities frame.
> 'Keep, ancient lands, your storied pomp!' cries she
> With silent lips. 'Give me your tired, your poor,
> Your huddled masses yearning to breathe free,
> The wretched refuse of your teeming shore.
> Send these, the homeless, tempest-tost to me,
> I lift my lamp beside the golden door!'[18]

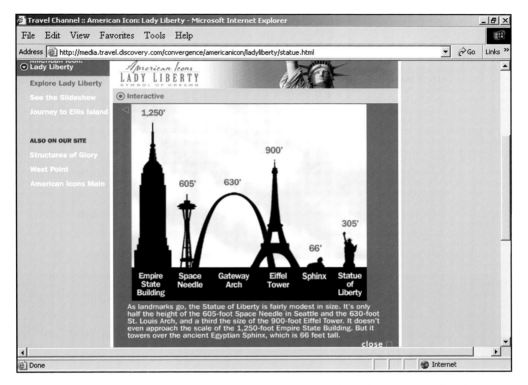

Travel Channel :: American Icon: Lady Liberty - Microsoft Internet Explorer

File   Edit   View   Favorites   Tools   Help

Address   http://media.travel.discovery.com/convergence/americanicon/ladyliberty/statue.html   Go   Links »

Lady Liberty

Explore Lady Liberty
See the Slideshow
Journey to Ellis Island

ALSO ON OUR SITE
Structures of Glory
West Point
American Icons Main

American Icons
LADY LIBERTY
SYMBOL OF DREAMS

Interactive

1,250'

900'

605'   630'

305'

66'

Empire   Space   Gateway   Eiffel   Sphinx   Statue
State   Needle   Arch   Tower   of
Building   Liberty

As landmarks go, the Statue of Liberty is fairly modest in size. It's only half the height of the 605-foot Space Needle in Seattle and the 630-foot St. Louis Arch, and a third the size of the 900-foot Eiffel Tower. It doesn't even approach the scale of the 1,250-foot Empire State Building. But it towers over the ancient Egyptian Sphinx, which is 66 feet tall.

close

Done   Internet

The Statue of Liberty is large for a statue, but is modest when compared with other famous landmarks.

President Calvin Coolidge declared the Statue of Liberty a national monument on October 15, 1924. In 1933, the National Park Service was put in charge of administration and maintenance of the statue. Since then, generations of people have enjoyed visiting the statue that was originally named "Liberty Enlightening the World."

Ellis Island Today

In 1965, Ellis Island was designated a national monument by President Lyndon B. Johnson. It became part of the Statue of Liberty National Monument, which is run by the National Park Service. However, the buildings remained in disrepair for over fifteen years.

▲ *After the immigration station was abandoned in 1954, it began to deteriorate. Plaster from the walls peeled off and beams rotted while rooftops caved in. Shown here is the Great Hall after it was renovated for the 1986 Statue of Liberty Centennial celebration.*

From 1976 to 1984, visitors were allowed into Ellis Island on a limited basis, but much of the grounds were in need of repair.[1] In the mid 1980s, plans were made to restore the buildings and create a museum that would be dedicated to the immigration experience. The Department of the Interior, which is in charge of the National Park Service, chose a private group to raise funds for the restoration and the construction of a museum. This group, called the Statue of Liberty–Ellis Island Foundation, raised the money for the project, as well as oversaw the restorations to make sure that the main building, which would be the home of the museum, was preserved as a landmark.

An Expensive Task

The project of restoring Ellis Island's main building took eight years and cost $156 million. It had been decided that the main building would be restored to its 1918 to 1924 period.[2] In the time that Ellis Island had been abandoned, many of the buildings had been ruined due to neglect. The roofs had rotted, saltwater had ruined the floors, and trees and weeds grew everywhere. The restoration team had an incredible amount of work to do.

It ended up being well worth it. On September 10, 1990, the Ellis Island Immigration Museum opened. The museum receives nearly 2 million visitors each year. On permanent display to relay the tales of American immigration are hundreds of photos and thousands of artifacts. For example, in the Baggage Room there is a display of luggage that would have been used during that period of time. The museum also contains a children's interactive learning center.[3] Audio tours are available in six different languages.

During the cleanup process, some of the restorers noticed initials, dates, poems, cartoons, comments, and religious symbols drawn on the plaster of the walls in the main room. This room is known as the Registry Room or the Great Hall. These have been restored as well, and are also on view in the museum.

There are two theaters, both of which feature a documentary about the history of Ellis Island as an immigration station. The movie is called *Island of Hope, Island of Tears,* by David McCullough, which can also be ordered online or found at many local libraries. There are other types of informative and entertaining shows. One is a play called *Ellis Island Stories;* another is a one-person show called *Voices From the Past.* Visitors can also go to the "Oral History Library" and listen to interviews with people who passed through Ellis Island.

Located behind the main building on Ellis Island is the American Immigrant Wall of Honor, the largest wall of names in the world. Over five hundred thousand names are engraved into

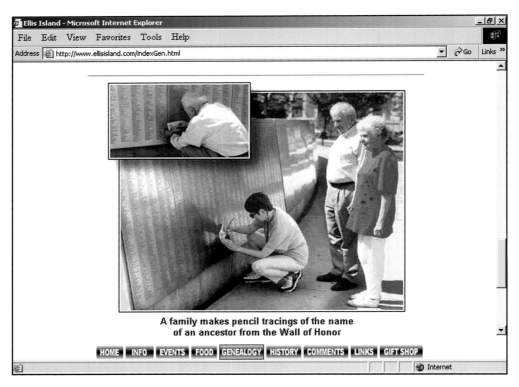

A family makes pencil tracings of the name
of an ancestor from the Wall of Honor

HOME   INFO   EVENTS   FOOD   GENEALOGY   HISTORY   COMMENTS   LINKS   GIFT SHOP

The American Immigrant Wall of Honor is the largest wall of names in the world. Families can pay a fee to have their ancestors' names inscribed on the Wall. It is very popular to make a rubbing of a name by placing a piece of paper over it and gently rubbing a pencil or crayon over the paper.

Immigrants line up to be inspected after arriving at Ellis Island.

the metal plates that make up the wall.[4] For around one hundred dollars, the names of your ancestors can be added to the wall. For greater contributions, the names receive special places of honor. There are over 100 million Americans who can trace their ancestry to someone who passed through Ellis Island. Could you be one of those people?

The Statue of Liberty Today

People now know that the environmental conditions surrounding the Statue of Liberty were harmful to its exterior. The salt in the air from the waters of New York Harbor was eroding the copper structure. In 1980, the statue's structure—both inside and out—was examined thoroughly. It was found that immediate steps

President Richard M. Nixon arrived on Liberty Island September 26, 1972, to dedicate the American Museum of Immigration. He was joined by Mrs. Nixon and New York children invited to the opening ceremonies, in costumes showing their families' ethnic origins. (Source: Photograph Collection of the American Museum of Immigration, Liberty Island, U.S. Department of the Interior, NPS)

▲ President Richard Nixon dedicated the American Museum of Immigration on September 26, 1972. This museum is housed within an addition made to the base of the statue, completed in 1965. Exhibits on immigration to the United States and its impact on the nation can be viewed there.

needed to be taken to prevent pieces of the statue from falling to the ground, possibly harming someone or damaging the pedestal. The inspectors also discovered that the statue's "ribs" were corroding and needed to be replaced, so a material called 316–L was chosen to replace the original iron. Due to the way it had been assembled, one of the points in the statue's crown had stabbed into its raised arm, and water was leaking into the statue through this hole. The torch had been damaged beyond repair, so the decision was made to remove it and put it on display within the statue. A new torch, designed using Bartholdi's original plans, would be created to replace the original one.

People Get Involved

President Ronald Reagan responded to these reports. He asked the head of the Chrysler Corporation, Lee Iacocca, to lead an effort to raise funds to refurbish the statue. The Statue of Liberty-Ellis Island Foundation was founded at this time. The goal of the foundation was to raise money to restore the statue so that it looked brand new.

Adjustments to the interior needed to be made as well. Air conditioning was installed for the comfort of the Statue of Liberty's many visitors during the summer months. A double-decker elevator was also installed, and the stairs were widened and repaired. The American Museum of Immigration was added to the pedestal. Exhibits featured there include photographs and other objects from the early days of immigration, as well as information about the statue itself, from concept to construction.[1]

The restoration of the Statue of Liberty was completed in 1986, in time for the one-hundredth anniversary of the dedication of the statue in the United States. The cost of the restoration was $86 million. On July 4, 1986, the fully restored Statue of Liberty was unveiled to America in a dramatic show of lights, with fireworks in the background. It had been one of the most challenging undertakings of its kind in American history. Millions of people

▲ Since it was unveiled in 1886, the Statue of Liberty has become a universal symbol of freedom and democracy.

visited the statue over the next fifteen years, eager to view the proud symbol of freedom.

The terrorist attacks on New York City's World Trade Center on September 11, 2001, caused the statue to be closed. The closure was due to the cost of the additional security that was required. At first, this was approximately $7 million. The National Park Service reopened the statue to the public on August 3, 2004. Visitors were no longer allowed to climb the steps or take elevators to near the top of the statue. Instead, a glass ceiling was constructed that allows tourists to view inside the statue. New lighting and a new video system have been installed. Rangers provide tours of the Statue of Liberty and the pedestal that it stands on. Visitors can also tour the museum and areas of what was Fort Wood. The observation deck is open to the public so that everyone can take in the breathtaking views of New York City.

Throughout the years, Ellis Island and America's gift from France have stood as a proud reminder of the values for which our ancestors fought, so that we might enjoy the many advantages this country has to offer. As long as the Ellis Island Immigration Museum stands and the Statue of Liberty has her place in the water, we will always remember the freedom upon which our country was founded and the people who came here in pursuit of that dream.

ammunition—Projectiles, such as bullets or shot, that are fired from a gun.

barracks—A building or group of buildings that are used to house soldiers or military personnel.

bathhouse—A structure used for bathing or containing dressing rooms that people can change in after bathing.

deportation—The formal removal of a foreign national who is in violation of immigration laws.

dormitory—A residence hall containing living quarters.

enlightenment—The act of gaining knowledge or insight.

gibbet—Also called a gallows, these were posts that used to be used to hang criminals.

immigration—The movement of people from one country to another country.

landmark—A building or structure of historical importance.

persecution—The act of causing someone to suffer because of his or her race, religion, or social beliefs.

prosperity—A condition of success and good fortune.

quarantine—The isolation of a sick person to prevent the spread of a contagious disease.

restoration—To bring something back to its original condition.

Statue of Liberty and Ellis Island Facts

1. U.S. Department of the Interior, "Statue of Liberty," *National Park Service,* n.d., <http://www.nps.gov/stli/> (September 10, 2004).

2. Pamela Reeves, *Ellis Island: Gateway to the American Dream* (New York: Michael Friedman Publishing Group, 1991), p. 9.

3. Ibid., p. 70.

Chapter 1. Coming to America

1. A&E Television Networks, "The History of Ellis Island," 1998–2004, <http://www.historychannel.com/ellisisland/index2.html>(June 30, 2003).

2. "Ellis Island History," *Ellis Island Immigration Museum,* 2002, <http://www.ellisisland.com/inspection.html> (June 30, 2003).

3. Ibid.

4. David M. Brownstone, Irene M. Franck, and Douglass L. Brownstone, *Island of Hope, Island of Tears* (New York: Rawson, Wade Publishers, 1979), p. 144.

5. A&E Television Networks, "The History of Ellis Island," 1998–2004, <http://www.historychannel.com/ellisisland/whoare/index.html> (June 30, 2003).

6. Pamela Reeves, *Ellis Island: Gateway to the American Dream* (New York: Michael Friedman Publishing Group, 1991), pp. 61–62.

7. Ibid.; Nancy Foner, *From Ellis Island to JFK: New York's Two Great Waves of Immigration* (New Haven, Conn.: Yale University Press, 2002), p. 78.

Chapter 2. History of Ellis Island

1. American Park Network, "History: Ellis Island," 2001, <http://www.americanparknetwork.com/parkinfo/sl/history/ellis.html> (June 3, 2003).

2. Andrea Temple and June F. Tyler, "Americans All: A National Education Program," n.d., <http://americansall.com/PDFs/02-americans-all/12.9.pdf> (July 30, 2003).

3. Columbia University's Graduate School of Journalism, "Beyond Manhattan," May 2003, <http://newmedia.jrn.columbia.edu/2003/islands/index.html> (July 28, 2003).

4. Pamela Reeves, *Ellis Island: Gateway to the American Dream* (New York: Michael Friedman Publishing Group, 1991), p. 31.

5. PageWise Inc., "Ellis Island History," 2002, <http://tn.essortment.com/ellisislandhis_rqrb.htm> (August 1, 2003).

6. Reeves, p. 70.

7. B. Colin Hamblin, "Ellis Island," n.d., <http://sydaby.eget.net/swe/ellis_island.htm> (July 20, 2003).

8. Reeves, p. 91.

9. Hamblin, "Ellis Island."

10. University of Maryland Libraries, "Ellis Island," 2001, <http://www.lib.umd.edu/NTL/ellis.html> (August 1, 2003); The National Park Service, "Ellis Island History," *Statue of Liberty National Monument and Ellis Island,* September 7, 2004, <http://www.nps.gov/stli/serv02.htm> (July 31, 2003).

Chapter 3. History of the Statue of Liberty

1. American Park Network, "History: Statue of Liberty," 2001, <http://www.americanparknetwork.com/parkinfo/sl/history/liberty.html> (August 1, 2003).

2. Frank Spiering, *Bearer of a Million Dreams: The Biography of the Statue of Liberty* (Ottawa, Ill.: Jameson Books, Inc., 1986), p. 141.

3. Gary Feurstein, "Statue of Liberty Facts," *The Statue of Liberty*, October 20, 2001, <http://www.endex.com/gf/buildings/liberty/libertyfacts.htm> (July 23, 2003).

4. Spiering, p. 153.

5. "History: Statue of Liberty."

6. Jonathan Harris, *A Statue for America: The First 100 Years of the Statue of Liberty* (New York: Macmillan Publishing Company, 1985), p. 13.

7. Spiering, p. 156.

8. Harris, p. 73.

9. Ibid., p. 80.

10. Ibid., p. 104.

11. Ibid., p. 114.

12. The Library of Congress, "Today in History: Statue of Liberty," n.d., <http://memory.loc.gov/ammem/today/jun19.html> (June 19, 2003).

13. Ibid.

14. Leslie Allen, *Liberty: The Statue and the American Dream* (New York: Simon & Schuster, 1985), pp. 15–16.

15. Spiering, p. 53.

16. Aizenberg Yuri, "The Colossus of Rhodes," *The Seven Wonders of the Ancient World*, July 2002, <http://mars.netanya.ac.il/~aizeyuri/rodos.html> (August 1, 2003).

17. Ibid.

18. Harris, p. 88.

Chapter 4. Ellis Island Today

1. National Park Service, "Ellis Island History," *Ellis Island*, November 24, 2004, <http://www.nps.gov/stli/serv02.htm#Ellis> (December 14, 2004).

2. Pamela Reeves, *Ellis Island: Gateway to the American Dream* (New York: Michael Friedman Publishing Group, 1991), p. 125.

3. "Ellis Island History," Ellis Island Immigration Museum, 2002, <http://www.ellisisland.com/indexHistory.html> (August 1, 2003).

4. "American Family Immigration History Center," *The Statue of Liberty/Ellis Island Foundation*, 2000, <http://www.ellisisland.org> (May 23, 2004).

Chapter 5. The Statue of Liberty Today

1. "American Family Immigration History Center," *The Statue of Liberty/Ellis Island Foundation*, 2000, <http://www.ellisisland.org> (May 23, 2004).

Bial, Raymond. *Tenement: Immigrant Life on the Lower East Side.* Boston: Houghton Mifflin, 2002.

Curlee, Lynn. *Liberty.* New York: Athenum, 2000.

Deady, Kathleen W. *The Statue of Liberty.* Mankato, Minn.: Bridgestone Books, 2002.

Heinrichs, Anne. *The Statue of Liberty.* Minneapolis, Minn.: Compass Point Books, 2001.

Hopkinson, Deborah. *Shutting Out the Sky: Life in the Tenements of New York, 1880–1915.* New York: Orchard Books, 2003.

Knowlton, MaryLee and Dale Anderson. *Arriving at Ellis Island.* Milwaukee, Wis.: Gareth Stevens Publishing, 2002.

Lawler, Veronica. *I Was Dreaming to Come to America: Memories From the Ellis Island Oral History Project.* New York: Viking, 1995.

Marcovitz, Hal. *Ellis Island.* Broomall, Penn.: Mason Crest Publishers, 2002.

Meltzer, Milton. *The Story of the European Immigrants.* Tarrytown, N.Y.: Cavendish, Marshall Corporation, 2001.

Roberts, Russell. *The Statue of Liberty.* Farmington Hills, Mich.: Gale Group, 2002.

Sandler, Martin W. *Island of Hope: The Story of Ellis Island and the Journey to America.* New York: Scholastic, 2004.

Walsh, Frank. *New York City.* Milwaukee, Wis.: World Almanac Library, 2004.

Wepman, Dennis. *Immigration: From the Founding of Virginia to the Closing of Ellis Island.* New York: 2002.

Young, Robert. *A Personal Tour of Ellis Island.* Minneapolis, Minn.: The Lerner Publishing Group, 2001.

A

American Committee, 27–29
American Immigrant Wall of Honor, 38–39
American Museum of Immigration, 40–41

B

Baggage Room, 37
Bartholdi, Frédéric-Auguste, 23, 28, 30, 33, 41

C

Chippewa Indians, 15–16
Colossus of Rhodes, 34
Coolidge, Calvin, 35

D

de Laboulaye, Edouard-Rene Lefebvre,
      22–23, 27
deportation, 11–12
donations, 23, 27–31

E

East River, 19
Ellis, Samuel, 17
Ellis Island Immigration Museum, 37, 43
Ellis Island Immigration Station
      Board of Special Inquiry, 13
      closing, 20–21
      enlargement, 18–19
      fire, 18
      Great Hall, see *Registry Room*
      history, 15–21, 38
      inspection process, 11–14, 17–20
      medical examination, 11–12, 18–20
      Registry Room, 19–20, 36–37
      restoration, 37
Ellis Island Stories, 38

F

Flore, 31
Fort Gibson, 17
Fort Wood, 25, 43
France, 22–23, 29, 31, 43
French-American Union, 27, 29

G

General Services Administration, 21

H

Hudson River, 19
Hunt, Richard Morris, 28

I

Iacocca, Lee, 41
Isere, 31
Island of Hope, Island of Tears, 38

J

Johnson, Lyndon B., 21, 36

L

Lazarus, Emma, 33–34
Liberty Island, 11, 33

M

Moore, Annie, 16–17

N

names, 13–14
National Park Service, 21, 32, 35–37, 43
New York Harbor, 10, 25, 28, 31, 40
New York World, 29, 31
Nixon, Richard, 40

P

Paauw, Michael, 15–16
pedestal
      construction, 27, 29
      cost, 29
      fund-raising, 27–31, 33–34
Peterssen, Arne, 21
pirates, 16
Pulitzer, Joseph, 29, 31

Q

Quarantine Station, 19

R

Reagan, Ronald, 41
reasons for immigration, 11, 14

S

September 11, 2001, terrorist attacks, 43
Sons of the American Revolution, The, 29
Statue of Liberty
      construction, 26–27
      dedication, 32
      erosion, 40–41
      face, 24–25
      height, 27, 31
      history, 22–35
      inspiration, 23–25
      restoration, 41
      symbolism, 33–34, 42–43
      weight, 31
Statue of Liberty–Ellis Island Foundation,
      37, 41

T

"The New Colossus," 33–34

U

Udall, Stewart, 21

V

Voices From the Past, 38